A Writer's Vine

A Writer's Vine

Poems

Sylvia R. Cooper

Sylvia R. Cooper

Terry—
Thank you for your
many years of friendship—
so loving and caring—
I treasure.
love—
Sylvia
7/18/16

Chapbook Press

Schuler Books
2660 28th Street SE
Grand Rapids, MI 49512
(616) 942-7330
www.schulerbooks.com

ISBN 13: 9781943359240

Library of Congress Control Number: 2015959526

Grateful acknowledgement is made to *The Banner*, in which the following poems first appeared: "Birth Day," "The Farewell," and "Who are You, Lord?"

Scripture taken from the Holy Bible, NEW INTERNATIONAL VERSION®, NIV® Copyright © 1973, 1978, 1984, 2011 by Biblica, Inc.® Used by permission. All rights reserved worldwide.

Printed in the United States by Chapbook Press.

For Catherine
who first saw
the cup of possibility

Contents

A Writer's Vine

Opening a Book 3
Book Store 4
The Art of a Poem 5
Soda Pop Words 6
Word Shapes 7
Word Twins 8
Word Flight 9
Getting Ahead of Myself 10
August Elegy 11
The Poet's Time 12
A Writer's Vine 13

Time Will Tell

Dandelions 17
The Seasons 18
So Much Change 20
The Twister 22
Windows 23
My Watch 24
Grief's Time 25
Morning's Mourning 26
Time Will Tell 27
The Hour Glass 28
The Fabric of Life 29
The Victory Tree 30
Revelation 31

The Vine and Branches

The Vine and Branches 35
The Zipper 36
The Marriage Candle 37
Birth Day 38
Millennium Music 39
Braids 40
The Gift 42
The Old Shoe 43
Folding Clothes 44
The Farewell 46
The Star 48
Supper Table 49
Her Feast 50
New Birth 52
The Cottage: Word Quiet 54

Feed My Lambs

Feed My Lambs 59
Flame in the Night 61
Drop File 63
The Robot 64
In Search of a Queen 65
Wussup? 66
Squid Out of Water 67
Child's Play 68
The Real Darryl 69
In the Deep of the City 70
The Sound Bassoonist 71

Enfolded

The Sentence 75
Who Are You, Lord? 76
flooded 78
Enfolded 79
Precipitation 81
Advent 82
Winter Blessing 83
His Light Presents 84
Today's Tomorrow 85

At the Threshold

At the Threshold 91

Notes 93
Acknowledgements 96
About the Author 101

A Writer's Vine

Opening a Book

Opening a book
is opening a door
to a world
where you can walk
the road of words
to become the sage,
the hero or the fool,
or just the I upon a wall
and still return
to sit and smile
at the adventure
that lingers
in your mind
and heart.

Book Store

It's a forest
of deep, painted browns and greens.
The bookshelves stand
in lines like saplings on a tree farm,
each stack waiting for the market's harvest.

In small clearings, large soft chairs
beckon wanderers to pick from a tree.
"Paradise," Adam whispers to Eve
who opens the leaves of a book
to taste its fruit.

The Art of a Poem

Some poems paint a picture
my mind can hold;
some poems sing a song
my heart can hear.

But some poems mold
mind and heart together
into a glass
my soul can fill.

Soda Pop Words

Some words are as sweet
as soda pop.

When you drink them,
they tickle your nose,
sizzle in your ear,
burn your eyes—

then numb your tongue
and throat,
bloat your stomach—

leaving you thirsty
for pure filtered water
but addicted
to that saccharine
soda pop taste.

Word Shapes

To poets, words are books—
each with its own story,
look and feel;
books a poet can page through:
touching, trying all the meanings—
flat or round or sharp,
soft or hard, prickly or smooth—
looking for the shape of the perfect line.

To philosophers, words are blocks
of brushed steel with sides
that interlock neat and clean
so sentences can be
built clear and distinct—
strong as a concrete wall.

To children, words are flowers
to be picked and enjoyed,
put into colorful bouquets
and given to someone they love.

But to most, words are words—
what they say, read, or write—
names of things—
firm as a handshake—but shapeless
as wind-driven smoke.

Word Twins

Kind is a twin like two bricks
that look and sound the same
but show different sides
when built into a sentence wall.

Word Flight

In the back of my middle-aged brain
I see words
fluttering beyond my grasp
like Monarch butterflies dancing
on a summer breeze
beyond my porch.

Some words test me—
like the large fly that struts up my arm
buzzes around my head
until it lands on my blank page
and stares up at me
with a teasing challenge
in its eyes.

Getting Ahead of Myself

When my story gets snowed in,
the self that gets tired
of shoveling through the details
flies ahead in news-copter style
over piled-up drifts
to predict
the traffic pattern
for the tale
left behind in the cold.

August Elegy

Although it is not quite Labor Day,
I glean words I planted in May.
I retreat to the back porch,
take a pen,
and place a garden invoice
backside up
on a volume of *Poetry Speaks*.
But words
hide like the pole beans
that wound their long tendril-thin arms
around the beef steak tomato plants.
Only the white-flag bean blossoms
signal where the next fruit will be.
Otherwise all are lost in the green leaves
as the cicadas sing of summer's end.

The Poet's Time

Her voice is a sea
standing in the wake of time:
her silver sentence rides the wave's blade
that cuts the present,
and her cold water words course
the currents
that press the past,
while her semantic tide combs the shore
that holds the future.

A Writer's Vine

The piles of paper
growing on the spare bed
along the headboard
over the mound of pillows
and zig-zagging
across the open spread
down towards the foot
are like
the squash vine
meandering
down the garden hill
along the white picket fence:
A few flashes of yellow buds
barely brighten the greens of leaves,
grass, and weeds,
with the suggestion of fruit.
But one modest flower
is opening
like a star-shaped cup
of possibility.

Time Will Tell

Dandelions

Today is
gone like dandelion puffs
blown by a child.

Catch the wind
seed my mind

with pictures of this moment's flower
cluttering my thoughts
as full and bright
as yellow weeds in a deep green lawn.

The Seasons

Spring is nature's childhood.
Winter's bare gray
gives birth to virgin green,
innocent to the intruding frost.
Soon tiny pastel lips open
where summer's fruit will be born.
In its adolescent dance
colors deepen into a vibrant palette,
vulnerable to this season's extremes,
but secure in its promise.

Summer is the young adult
that burns hot with flaming color
bursting with bright, plump offspring
surrounded by full-grown green.

Autumn is middle-aged maturity
nature is growing towards.
It arrives in a bold statement
dyed deep gold, crimson, and scarlet,
brightened by yellow and orange,
and tempered with rich browns.

Winter is the senior season:
cool, rainy winds sing
a proud song of barn-filled harvests
through gray, bare branches
and dried grasses

until the cold, winter white
covers nature's weary heart
where green seeds rest,
hidden,
waiting for their birth
into a new, spring world.

So Much Change

To a child
dimes and dollars,
a minute or an hour
are all the same—depending
on where they're spent—
church, McDonald's, or the store.

A youth
counts every dollar
of allowance into a jean pocket.
Who has time for pennies anymore?
To pinch or save in pigs or wallets or banks?
Tomorrow will always bring more welcome change.

A young adult
keeps playing Monopoly or Life,
incurring and paying debt
passing "Go" to thirty
betting on a salary
to survive the next plastic panic.

A middle-aged adult
spends the least and the most:
debits and credits add up
to an accounting crisis—
sometimes short and sometimes long.
Now or never,
they're ready to lose or save the whole account.

A senior
spends threescore and ten
like so much change—
dimes, nickels, quarters, a penny here and there.
Hours add up to days as slowly as life insurance matures
until minutes
fly like dollars in a department store sale
just before closing.

The Twister

Today is a twist of tomorrow and a tongue

of yesterday: it tells a tiny tale,

a tall tongue-twister

t e l l i n g

too much

or no-

thing

at

all.

Windows

The waiting room has no windows
except for the TV in the corner.
The room is quiet
except for Rachael Ray
telling her guests what to do with the worst gift
they've ever received.

Some women waiting here for mammograms
have like me
returned after cancer.
I see into their eyes
past wide, glassy TV-stares:
picture windows into a cancer ward.

My Watch
Ps. 90:12

To check the time
in my rush to work,
I glance down at my wrist.
Bare.
A wave of uneasiness
flows through me
like a shudder
at losing
my gold band
with its comforting analog face
ticking off
each second, minute, and hour.

I watch
my day
freed from the manacle
and gain
much more than time
in the end.

Grief's Time

for my parents

The sun moves on;
the shadows stay—
lengthening
the grave's monumental
reminder.

The clock turns
its hands
with no consideration
of what's been
left behind
as its gears slowly wind—
measuring life
but never
death's daily
remainder.

Morning's Mourning

In the morning
as I open the back door,
the spring breeze shakes
the leafy hands of the maple tree
sings through the screen,
and announces her arrival like an old friend.

As I turn on the TV
and open the door to the world—
victims of tornadoes, earthquakes, typhoons,
bombs, and drive-by shootings
cry out through the screen—
and I mourn their loss like lost friends.

Time Will Tell

The grim reaper left
his calling card inscribed on my face.

Among the folds and wrinkles, he pressed
my story, one line upon another.

Around my mouth, he carved a frown
of punch lines from life's bad jokes.

But in my smile, I left him
the revision grace has written over time.

The Hour Glass

I sit on the edge
of tomorrow,
and sink in the cool wave
pouring over my feet.

I scramble back against the glass
of the present
and toe the future
falling on my feet
like broken surf.

Here, I wait to step into tomorrow
and sink in its changing sands.

As I watch the steady flow
of grains
filling this glass shore,
I dig in my heels
against the fall
of every moment.

The Fabric of Life

Each day
is draped
upon me
like a long piece of fabric
placed in neat folds
around my shoulders.

One flows over me like bridal chiffon,
another weighs me down like wet wool,
one confines me like stiff taffeta and netting,
another cushions and insulates me
like quilted cotton batting:

all are sewn
into everyday clothing—
layers
woven and tailored
to fit me.

The Victory Tree

One side of the trunk
of the basswood tree
is perfectly rounded ,
full and muscular,
like a super hero
with a brawny arm
pointing up
to the forest canopy
and the light.

The other side
is half-gone
as if blown out
by an IED:
most of its bark
and inner core
are stripped away
right down
to its sawdust-covered
roots.

But that leafy limb
raised to heaven
waves in the breeze
like a victor's flag
held high by a soldier
just home from the war.

Revelation

It appears like snow
falling only
in my back yard
on a sunny October day,
unexpected
as an intruder
stealing my attention
away from my supper.

Like a child doubting
the magic of card tricks,
I wonder, "How can this be?"
Summer in my neighbor's garden;
winter in mine.

Through the window glass
I see
a white column of flakes
falling from heaven.

I go out into the cloud of light
to touch the heavenly down,
reaching up
to accept the gift.

The Vine and Branches

The Vine and Branches

Grapevines wrap their tendrils
around whatever they grow next to,
winding in and through it,
holding on,
two becoming one.

Branch knots to branch
one to another,
child to parent
brother to sister,
knitted to the vine—
family-tied.

The Zipper

A-   part
they match   each other.
Their love   links them
like a zip-   per slider,
filling the emp-   ty spaces
and joining   their metal
together.
Their promises
like zipper
stops--hold
the two
interlocked
from top
to bottom.

The Marriage Candle

Two lives glow   like two wicks:
       two cords   two flames
             moving   toward
                 each   other
           bonding binding
                 burning
                   like
           a spiral candle
       waxing long together—
                 one.

Birth Day

A wet, wailing black-haired boy
still kicking as I put him to my breast:
"Drink," I coax. "There. Now rest, my joy."
I wonder: What kind of treasure chest
is this? (I trace his lips.) Pandora's box?
Aladdin's lamp? Gently, I stroke his hair,
lest he know the fears a mother locks
within her heart. I think, "How do I dare
dream of the future?" But then, in his sleep
his lips curl up, as if to say,
"Don't worry, Mom." And I laugh deep
like Sarah doubting God's waiting way
of making gems. I sigh, kiss him,
and whisper, "You're my Isaac—not a whim."

Millennium Music

2000

Time is a song—
ever changing
its pulse and pitch,
pulling our ears to listen
and our hearts to sing.

The future sounds
like "Stairway to Heaven."
The past
like "Sesame Street."
The present
like "Time Is on My Side."

Music for a millennium
lasts for a thousand years
as if it were a day.
It plays in your soul
as surely
as picking the strings of a guitar
or plucking those of a viola—

because it's a love song,
        titled
"Immanuel—
God is with us all"—
sung from generation
to generation.

Braids

for my mother

As I braid my daughter's hair, I remember
my mother braiding mine, the pulling and tugging
of the brush—the comb straightening

the snarls, tangles, and knots. I still know
which sections of hair she parted off and which
I held while she began to weave the wispy

shortest strands on the sides, those most likely
to get lost. I know this ritual as well as my place
next to my father at the supper table. I remember

while Mom worked, I silently chanted: "Mother,
father, child. This will take a while." She braided,
taking one, then another from my hands,

weaving them close as a family so they would last
the day and the night. But the teasing pull of others
the stubborn shake and sleepy toss of my head

loosened even the tightest braids, pulling
apart like unforgiving parents and children.
Only the plait at the top, still held;

sometimes the rubber bands and even the ribbons
were lost, and stray ends stuck out rebelliously.
But in the morning, Mom took the braids all out

and brushed my hair again. In the hand mirror
she gave me, I saw the crimping of the weave:
the waves gave body the strands didn't have.

Now, as my mother did, I gather and part
the strands, giving my daughter bunches to hold
as I braid her hair tight to last the new day.

The Gift

Trillium—
white three-petal star
punctuated with a tiny pastel sun
collared with three small tongues of green
framed by three leafy palms
all supported
on one slender stem—

a daughter's colored-pencil picture
of love's resurrection light.

The Old Shoe

As soon as his father walks in the door,
the child asks,
"Dad, you going to play with me after supper?"
"What about Mom?" Dad raises his eyebrows to her.
"I'm the old shoe, remember?" she says
with a squinty smile.

Worn, stepped on, and dirty—
the old running shoe lies kicked off
beside the child's bed. The laces
hang untied with tips frayed
from being pushed through the eyes
again and again. Toe-holes lie
like open mouths of sleeping children.
Inside, footprints are molded into the sole—
those flat plains of newness
worn into rounded valleys of wear—
grown into, not out of. Used
like the teddy bear he carries everywhere.

Folding Clothes

Here are my children's clothes
washed and done.
Here are my children's days
folded into one.

As I fold clothes, I quickly sort
socks, pants, shirts.
In my haste I drop the number shirt
my nine-year-old quarterback wore
in his backyard game.
I retrieve it and hold it up:
he stands in front of me
in his faded, grass-stained jeans.
Watching the neighborhood game,
from my grand-stand window,
I cheer him on
as he runs for his touchdown.

Here are my children's clothes
washed and done.
Here are my children's days
folded into one.

I refold his shirt and tuck it away in his drawer,
my own keepsake box.

In the laundry basket
I see the sea-green bathing suit
my five-year-old mermaid wore
for her scales and fins:

my Ariel stands in front of me
in her wet, sand-covered suit.
Watching her play
from my reserved window seat,
I cheer her on
as she defeats the sea witch.

Here are my children's clothes
washed and done.
Here are my children's days
folded into one.

I quickly refold the suit
and place it in her drawer,
my private memory chest,
so I can finished the laundry
and get on
to peel potatoes for supper.

The Farewell

for my parents

If only I lived closer,
I would visit you
every week instead of
once a year.

I would drop in for coffee and windmill cookies,
take you to get your hair done at Terry's,
then to Burger King
for your fish sandwich and apple pie.

I'd play "Have Thine Own Way, Lord"
on your electric keyboard,
and together
we'd sing it loud and long.

If only I lived closer,
had a good back,
and didn't have arthritis,
I'd make your "Grandma's Goulash" for supper,
scrub your kitchen floor on my hands and knees,
wash your sheets and hang them outside,
then make your bed with firmly folded corners.

I'd push your wheelchair,
help you to the bathroom,
and put on your elastic socks.

If only I lived closer,
didn't have a job
and my own husband and children,
I would be all that you've been to me.

If only I lived closer…
I thought
as I waved goodbye to Mom and Dad,
who were standing by their dark red house.
"Wave!" I told my children. "Wave!
We don't know when we'll see them again!"

And we waved until
we turned the corner
down the hill
toward the interstate.

The Star

for my mother-in-law

She is the star
who brightened everyday things:
    feeding the ducks or stray cats,
    folding wash or clearing the table,
    singing around the piano,
    or watching lake liners.

She is the star
who brought a ray of Christmas to every season:
    sending her Dear Ones a few dollars,
    playing checkers with her Chicks,
    taking them to the pool or miniature golf,
    and never missing a birthday
    with at least a gift-stuffed card.

She is also the sun,
Christ-like,
who gathered all of us
    under her mother-hen wings:
    leaving our rough edges in the shadows,
    helping each one of us to shine
    and feel like her only star.

Supper Table

Grace is a table
extended
for the family meal
always growing
giving
making room
for more.

Her Feast

for Ev Hamstra

"Don't fuss," we'd told her.
"Use paper plates. We'll bring the food."
After all, we were her church family.

But when we came to her modular
retirement home, she had the table covered
with a linen tablecloth. Her china dishes
were surrounded by her silverware,
wine and water goblets, and cloth napkins—
placed like a quiet embrace. It was set
as if it were a banquet, a farewell banquet.

"How are you?" she greeted us, wrapping
her arms around each of us like a mother
and putting her good ear close to our words.

Together we filled the salad dishes
and cut the lasagna we'd brought;
she poured her wine. Then we all sat down
and she said grace.

While we ate, we remembered
how she had always brought meals
to sick church members and inner city friends.
We laughed as we retold the story
how she and her husband donated their garden
harvest to poor neighbors
until the church started its own food program.

Every week she helped sort out rotten potatoes,
cut pink rot from lettuce,
and listened to the stories of those who waited.
She did it all until her cancer came.

We nodded to each other
as we saw the tiredness spread over her face.
She allowed us to clear the table, wash up,
and put the extra chairs in the bedroom.
Then we left, filled with her feast.

New Birth

for Minnie Hunderman

She was like an aunt to me
in our small church group.
She prayed through my infertility
and I prayed for her healing.

Once a week
I came to her house
to eat supper together
to visit and wait.

We waited
as a baby grew in my stomach
and a tumor in hers.
We prayed for
what we were expecting.

Each week I silently watched
and compared our changes.
Then, she named them:
"We both have enlarged stomachs
and eat small meals.
We move awkwardly
and have shortness of breath."
I closed my eyes
to her vision.
"It'll be all right," she said
with a look of a seer
who is close to God.

When I gave birth to a healthy girl,
she said, "My prayers have been answered."

Three days later
she lay like a new born
in a mahogany-covered bed—
resting peacefully
cradled in arms of light.

The Cottage: Word Quiet

After supper
as we think over the next word for Scrabble,
muse through *Home* or *Sailing Grace*,
decipher the Sunday puzzle,
or peruse *Real Simple*—
a cloud of words
silently fills the family room
like water vapor,
and we rest together
in the fresh, *gezellig* rain
of friendship.

Feed My Lambs

Feed My Lambs

One night
while picking up the 12-year-olds
for girls' club,
it came as unexpected
as a rooster crowing in the city:
"Sylvia, do you love me?"

I knew who it was—
the only girl
who gave me a Christmas gift.
Weighing my words,
I checked my rear view mirror
but couldn't see her.

Then as if a deep well
had been tapped,
it flowed out:
"I love you.
I love all of you guys. That's why
I come and pick you up each week."
She was quiet. They were quiet.
She complimented her cousin on her braids.
She giggled. They giggled.

In my mouth there was a taste of bread,
warm and full of yeast
and in my ear hung the words:
Feed my lambs.

A month later on the ride home,
it came again—"Sylvia, do you love me?"

"Yes," I said, "I love you.
That's why I come and pick you up each week."
She was quiet. They were quiet.
She asked her cousin about her nails.
She giggled. They giggled.

I found myself sitting on a beach
with the taste of fish in my mouth
and the words hanging in my ear:
Feed my lambs.

Flame in the Night

We went to my house
to talk about her school work.
My words seemed as dull
as the reading she didn't do.

"You know I pray for you."
"Why? Because you my tutor lady?"

She laughed behind her hand
at the title she'd given to me,
her mentor
and academic cheerleader.

"No, because I care.
I pray for everybody I care for,
even people I don't care for."

I drove her home
in the silence of impending dusk.

"Don't forget to pray for me."
"No chance of that."

Hugging her books,
she got out and shuffled to her house—
shift-work empty.

She disappeared into its shadow.
I waited.
Suddenly she flung the door
open into the darkness.
She waved, smiling
like a flame in the night.

Drop File

I check Drop
on the Attendance Sheet,
write his name,
      then hers.

They've come and gone
like starlings
feeding on my mock orange bush.
Now, as if migration season has arrived,
they've gone to a warmer place—
where the snacks are all sugar,
the trips are always overnight,
and the leaders never say "No."

I place the form in the Drop folder.
Their faces hang in my heart
like pictures on a mother's bracelet.

I see
his baggy-pants swagger
and her tight-jeans stance
and smile.

I close the folder and file it:
I lift them up to you, O Lord.

The Robot

She lives in the passive voice
as if controlled by remote.
She answers
in short monotones
and shrugs.

All mechanics,
metal covering
of a tender
child.

In Search of a Queen

She kept
her beauty
close to her heart
like a priceless locket.

But one night she displayed
her true radiance.
When one of the girls slipped on the ice
and the others ran past their fallen cousin
to the van to claim their favorite seats,

she stopped
to help the girl,
not in her clique.

That's when
I saw
the heart of a queen--
the crown jewel
of Cinderella
and Mufaro's beautiful daughter.

Wassup?

What's that attitude
hangin' in your face?
You got lead in your soul?
Is it school
or somethin' real heavy
pullin' you down—
somethin' that won't let you lift
the law of the hood
from your heart?

Squid Out of Water

The student
slithered
into the room
dragging
and flinging
his rubbery limbs
like a squid
trying to swim through air.

A seaweed-green hue
grew over his face
as he smiled weakly at me
with a watery roll
of his bloodshot eyes
and slurred,
"S-s-orry, 'um late,
Ms. S-Sylvia,
missed-da-bus."

Child's Play

At the bus stop by the park, I heard
three twelve-year-old boys talking in a huddle
as if they were comparing basketball scores:
"They always shoot you in the chest.
That's what they do on TV," said one
I knew from Vacation Bible School.
"I know somebody who got shot in the face,"
said another who had D.A.R.E.
printed on his T-shirt.
"Well, I ain't gonna get shot," said the third.

"How do you know that?" I asked.
All three glared at me
as if I were a cop checking IDs.
"How do you keep from getting shot?"
"You run in a church
or somewhere safe," the first boy said.
"You don't do drugs," answered the second.
But the third turned away like a scolded child
and swaggered into the park to the jungle gym
where he hung upside down
with his knees hooked over a bar.

The bus came.
The boys climbed on the bus
that would bring them to the magnet school
for the gifted and talented.

The Real Darryl

for Darryl

His full Phat Boy smile
is like a light
from a door left ajar
that floods a dark hall.

When he first walks into the computer lab
with his twelve-year-old buddies,
a ready-to-play energy radiates from him.

"Darryl Weaver." I check the name off.
"No. Walker."
I raise my brows.
He beams.
"Okay, Darryl Walker gets the rewards."
"Aw, Ms. Sylvia, "I'm just playin'.""
I grinned. "I know. Good thing I know
the real Darryl."

Years later
that's how I remember him:
a true light—
snuffed out too soon
by a drive-by shooter.

In the Deep of the City

I know children in the deep
of the city who grow where they can
like chicory squeezing up
between the sidewalk cracks
in front of abandoned stores
where spray-painted graffiti announces
"Thuggin for life" one day, and proclaims
"huggin for life" the next.

I know children in the drought
of the city who squat
like street musicians in church doorways
and call out to strangers
to watch their show —
where they leap up in the air,
flip mid-jump and land on their feet
like cats in the grass.

And I know children in the dust
of the city who wait for a word of applause
like weeds wilted from the heat
waiting for a drink
to quench their thirst
where roots hold their ground —
so they can grow, huggin for life
like chicory after a summer rain.

The Sound Bassoonist

Strong and complex
with a deep mellow tone,
the bassoon
is basic to the woodwind family

like you
who
    without the usual
    means and support

chose to play the unusual
with a steady robust air

that kept you in tune
to the conductor's direction

with sound
first-chair success.

Enfolded

The Sentence

As if from Eden's tree—words failed:
silent angels stood before the gate;
the woman groaned in her delivery;
and love's quiet face told a stony tale:

here I, Eve, stood alone—
quietly seeing, quietly breathing,
quietly feeling, knowing the pain—
and I lay down in dust and ashes, waiting

to hear a woman like me sing—
"the Mighty One has done great things
for me—holy is his name…"
then nothing will be the same:

angels praise in the shepherd's light,
the child cries out his miracle,
and love commands the stone away—
as if from Eden's tree: the Word reigns.

Who are you, Lord?

I ask: Who are you, Lord?
Who are you in this unstable, debt-filled world?

I hear a still small voice:
I am the insurance agent who's paid
your premiums with interest,
and the bank manager who's paid
all your debt out of my own account.

I am the contractor who's building
your mansion, making it ready
for the time when our present
home falls apart and burns.

I ask: Who are you, Lord?
Who are you in this sterile, yet diseased world?

I hear the still small voice:
I am the doctor, the specialist
who examines you, diagnoses
your disease, and offers
the treatment and cure.

I am the nurse, the care-giver
who gives you transfusions,
who washes you all over
and rubs your back before you sleep.

I ask: Who are you, Lord?
Who are you in this "me-first" lonely world?

I hear the still small voice:
I am the father who fathered you,
who nurtures you with my Word:
I am the mother who bore you,
who nurtures you with my milk.

I am the family who opens
my home when you come—
who shares my supper
when you hunger and thirst.

Still, I ask: Who are you, Lord?
Who are you in this hurtful, violent world?

Still, I hear the still small voice:
I am the friend, the kindred spirit
who listens long; the one
whose lap you lay your head upon
and cry—when life's gone wrong.

I am the author, the composer
of a serenade—and the lover
who sings it passionately,
"Be still, and know that I am God."

flooded

i stand at my small window like Noah's wife
gazing at the rain for hours days weeks
that follow each other like a run on sentence
with no caps or punctuation

pouring through my moments
like the precipitation i have come to know
as well as the husband i find pacing
through paragraphs
on our slippery deck

cradled on the wind's waves
that smack my window
like a giant cloudy hand while we wait
for the end and the new world
that comes so slowly i begin to call myself
thomas the doubter
who believes in miracles only when she can touch

the evidence like a dove returning
with a dry olive leaf
not just the breaking clouds
refracting the light into a rainbow
like a giant parenthesis
or a mirror-image of a heavenly smile

as i stand at my small window like Noah's wife

Enfolded

Wounded and weary,
I wander alone
like a sheep in bitter pastures
while the wind whispers:

Where's your Shepherd and his fold?

Didn't his rod and staff
comfort you?
Didn't his food and drink
nourish you?

Don't you hear his voice?
Don't you see his face?

Where's your Shepherd and his fold?

He finds me where I wander.
He calls me by name and tends my wounds.

He leads me home.
His word feeds me at supper
when he lifts up the fruit
of the vine and grain.

Now I hear:
I am the good Shepherd
who lays down his life for his
sheep.
Now I see:
He is my Shepherd
who enfolded me.

Precipitation

A Prayer

Lord, come to me
in sprinkles—
little eyelets that spill
into rivulets,
tearing the dust
from my face.

Lord, come to me
in droplets—
tiny prisms on my lenses
that separate the light
into rainbows
I can see.

Lord, come to me
in summer showers—
gentle rain
that waters my garden,
fills its well
and quenches my thirst.

Lord, come to me
in a deluge—
a cloudburst of living water
that falls heavy and hard
 to wash, plant, and feed
your garden within me.

Advent

Stop the sun!
Hold on to this little light.
December gray broke today
and eclipsed my plans
of hibernation.
I ran outside
to harvest this day's last light.

But in going out and looking up,
I found the lasting light:
the largest star,
the brightest sun.

Winter Blessing

When cold nights grow long,
your love comes to me like snow
gently billowing down
on an almost windless day.
The lacy flakes cover me
like white petit point thread
on a dark blue canvas.

In this bold bright pattern
before the bite and numbness come,
my nerve ends tingle as if pricked
and awakened by tiny needles.

Within this billowing art
I lift up my hands
and catch one delicate gift.
In my palm
I see your present,
the intricate design you've sewn—
new and different
pure and light
given
only to be renewed
again and again.

His
Light
Presents

Advent promises

the light will come,

dispelling all shadows.

Even the darkness between us

will be ripped away like tissue paper

wrapped around a present placed under

a tree but never truly given, opened, or seen.

Through Epiphany the Christ child guides all wise

travelers to the house where they give their gifts. There

he receives and unwraps each one. As our Morning Star

he reveals

each present's light.

Today's Tomorrow

A Contemporary Psalm

Look to the Lord, all you people.
Look to the Lord, all you who gather in this place.

Neighborhoods, youth, and programs
Belong to God. Praise him all you peoples.
Today's memory begets tomorrow's vision.
The Lord is our builder, keeper, and guide.

Look to the Lord.
Celebrate his goodness.
See what he has done.

He summoned pastors and planners
And guided them to this place.
He opened ears to the knocks on the church door
And to the calls from parish porches.

He gathered children from this neighborhood.
He collected them like a mother
Who calls her children home,
Who protects and keeps them safe.

He chose leaders
To love and nurture city kids
To teach them to be his children
And grow in his grace.

He built his web
From one church to another
Until youth programs
Stretched from eastside to west.

Look to the Lord.
Celebrate his goodness.
See what he has done
Look what he will do:

The Lord will build his kingdom.
He will keep his people strong,
He will guide them in his ways.
For the Lord keeps his promises
Yesterday, today, and tomorrow.

Look to the Lord, all you people.
Look to the Lord, all you who gather in this place.

Neighborhoods, youth, and programs
Belong to God. Praise the Lord.

Today's memory begets tomorrow's vision.
The Lord is our builder, keeper, and guide.

At the Threshold

At the Threshold

The last page
of a book is
a threshold
where you can open
or close a door,
return
or leave—
where you can see
within
and beyond,
the beginning
as well as the end.

Notes

"My Watch" p. 24

Psalm 90:12 "Teach us to number our days aright, that we may gain a heart of wisdom." *The Holy Bible, New International Version*. Grand Rapids: Zondervan Publishing House, 1973.

"Millenium Music" p. 39

Stanza 2   music my children listened to:

Line 2—song by Led Zeppelin

Line 4— Sesame Street theme song

Line 6— song by the Rolling Stones

Stanza 3

Lines 6-7—instruments my children play

Stanza 4

Line 3—name from Isaiah 7:14; Matthew 1:23

Line 4—Grandma Cooper's last words

"The Cottage: Word Quiet" p. 54

Line 9—The word *gezellig* is Dutch for enjoyable, cozy, or sociable.

"Feed My Lambs" pp. 59-71

I wrote the poems in this section in response to my work as a leader of the GEMS Girls' Club and as Tutor Coordinator of W.E.B. Tutoring. Both of these programs serve low income inner city children and are ministries of Eastern Avenue Christian Reformed Church.

"In Search of a Queen" p. 65
>Stanza 4: Line 6—*Mufaro's Beautiful Daughters* by John Steptoe is a picture book of an African Cinderella story.

"In the Deep of the City" p. 70
>This poem was the first I wrote (1994) about children in the Baxter neighborhood of Grand Rapids. The boys who played on the Parish House Office steps captured the hearts of all who passed.

>The poem appeared in an earlier form in *Inner City Church Tutoring: How to Administer and Train Tutors* (2005), p. 21. Neland Christian Reformed Church and Pathways to Possibilities of Calvin College requested that I write a tutoring manual for P2P member churches. P2P copied and distributed it. Retaining the copyright, I have continued to share this manual with other churches when requested.

"The Sentence" p. 75
>Stanza 3 lines 3-4—Luke 1:49.
>*The Holy Bible, New International Version.* Grand Rapids: Zondervan Publishing House, 1973.

"Today's Tomorrow" p. 85

I wrote this poem for a dinner celebrating W.E.B.
youth programs. These were neighborhood youth
programs of Wedgwood Christian Services as well
as Eastern Avenue Christian Reformed Church. I
was inspired by the theme of the dinner: an African
word, *sankofa*, which means, "Today's memory
begets tomorrow's vision."

Acknowledgments

I would like to thank the many people who have encouraged me, helped me to grow as a poet, and commented on this book as I prepared it for publishing.

I am grateful to my writer's group who encouraged me and helped me hone my skills. I especially would like to thank Barbara Carvill, Jane Griffioen, and Mary Vander Goot for their helpful suggestions on a final draft of the manuscript.

I truly appreciate the insightful comments of my friend Ruth Bolt who often has been the second reader of my work and was a reader of one of the final drafts.

I'm grateful to Meredith Post-Tremain who helped with some copy-editing decisions, layout, and design of the book.

I especially appreciate Alena Schuessler DeYoung, who copy-edited and formatted the manuscript in preparation for publication.

My husband, John, and my children, John and Catherine, read my poems, often more than once. I want to thank them for their honest, helpful encouragement, especially in continuing this project. My writing has improved because of it. I especially appreciate the support my husband has given me while I prepared this book for publication.

Lastly, I would like to thank my daughter, Catherine.
This book would not have been published if it were not
for her vision and initiative. In the fall of 2010 she secretly
printed this book in a similar form after carefully reading
and selecting poems from my files, organizing them into
sections, and designing the manuscript. She surprised
me with it on Christmas 2010. I did not have the words to
express my gratitude to her for such an extraordinary gift. I
hope the dedication is an apt expression of what it's meant
to me.

About the Author

Sylvia R. Cooper is a writer and retired teacher. After graduating from Calvin College in 1970 and teaching in Toronto, Canada, she moved to Grand Rapids, Michigan, where she pursued a master's degree, taught, and worked on several education projects. She also began to focus on writing poetry, a life-long interest, sharing with writer's groups, community, and family. She published in local journals.

For almost 20 years she developed and directed a church-based K–12 tutoring program for low income children in inner city Grand Rapids. Her students inspired her to write a number of poems, some included in this collection. After retiring in 2014, she has continued to write poetry and tutor students who struggle with reading.

She has two grown children and lives with her husband in Grand Rapids, Michigan.